An Iroy Nga Tuna (The Motherland), A Dedication

Mildred Grace German

BookLeaf Publishing

Presentation by *BookLeaf Publishing*

Web: www.bookleafpub.com

E-mail: info@bookleafpub.com

ISBN: 9789357213219

First edition 2023

I Long For You

Born and raised in the Philippines
A very beautiful warm country
since time immemorial
Kissed by the Sun in the Pacific
And there is a hum and a saying,
"You can take a girl out of the Philippines
But not the Philippines out of a girl".

An Iroy Nga Tuna: Land of Gold and Flowers

Land of gold and flowers
The love bestowed to her palms
Offering beauty and glow
Grace and perfect beauty
Nest of comfort and warmth

From the music of soothing breeze
The flow of the waters in my feet
The joy of visions in the horizons
Of clear skies, colorful hues
And all the shades of blues

An iroy nga tuna

Salted Red Eggs

At times of weaker economy
When there's no opportunity
To make ends meet, to eat and feed
In the uncertain times, challenging times
When hunger eats and hurts
Not only the body, but also the soul
Eggs, red eggs
Preserved eggs, salted eggs
Soaked in brine
Eggs covered in mud, this land
Flavours of the puddles of thick earth
Folded with salt from the ocean wide

Tactfully dipped in red-colored dyes
Red. Red in colour strong
Strength, fire, power, love
That willpower to survive, to thrive

Let's make ends meet
Let's dream more dreams
Dream a little dream, the impossible
When cities have no pities and care
Let's make ends meet, together

From zero to nothing to something
To have food on our empty plates
And shelter above our head
A peso, a penny, a dollar, a dream

I love to remember where I came from
The land, the water, the salt that seasons
I love to remember where I came from
Even in rainy stormy days
I love to remember where I came from
That bonded love---so strong

Obra Maestra.

The movement of clay
The pushing of dirt
Against my palms
Like a canvas and paint
In the bosom of a brush
Feeling the pastel and silk
Under my callous hands
Creating something wonderful
As wheels are spinning around
In a world that too spins with me
Give room for this wind of love
Under this same sun of fire that grazes
Spreading crystal-diamond stars
As clouds and rain, as everybody disappear
You. How amazing you astound!
Breathless; how we catch air
This burning rose heart will shine
As your eyes gaze to mine
This true love glazes you and I
Everlasting obra maestra

Cure the Malaise

It could be in a form of grieving for the world,
the unhappiness of the surrounding environment
internally and externally.

There are many roots and deeper symptoms
of malaise too, in economics, politics, identity,
and the chaos and limitations of the universe.

At the same time, cure can be painful.
At times, there can be no cure.
Denied. Deprived. Oppressed.
Do we evolve, acquire, grow, or retaliate,
live, or die...we are faced with whatever.
But the latter.

Labour Export

Many stories happen during
The height
Of the migrant labour needs
In this era of shortages
Of skilled workers,
Which the Labour Export Policy
Means trafficking of Filipino people
Into the diaspora to work
In over 156 countries
Around the world.

The era of export
Of the 10million Filipinos
In the modern era
Of the 20th and 21st centuries,
With ancestral roots
Of a Peoples' defiant struggle
And the ongoing stories
Of resistance and survival.

Art Of Hope

In critical times, art serves its purpose.
Art, as a form of hope,
Is reflected in the songs
Of birds chirping,
The sunrise, the sunset,
And the changing colors of the leaves.

There are many things around us
And beyond that remind us
Of the wonders
And chaos
Of life
Through art.

Art has been here since
Time immemorial.
The Creator must be an artist!
The Creator's glory is reflected
In the stars, the galaxies, the mountains,
The oceans, and more creations visible
And invisible to the naked eye.

Taking to heart an Art practice (or multiple)
Is one of the most wonderful feelings
In this universe.

Tedious

Waiting is tedious.
To pack up belongings.
Then to leave most
of the other
Belongings.
Including the lonely bench
Which got me used to being
Accompanied each day...

Everything In Sight

The moon is up in the sky,
She stares at the moon up above,
And thinks of her mother
---how soon they will be together again.

Just when the darkness arrives,
some fireflies pass by, and play by,
And gracefully dance.

With all the blinking stars
That are millions and millions
Of miles away. The emptiness
Of the void remains out there.
Out there.

Sky Wraps

The psychedelic stars
And constellations guide
Our walks as the darkness
Brings in the night
Out there with stars are up
In that unreachable void,
The evening sky wraps
The Pacific archipelago.
Galaxies' gems in this dark
Horizon.

Oh Mango

An Iroy Nga Tuna
Like a mango of golden sweetness
I long for you!
As a Filipino growing up in the province
Seeing the farmers' hard work in
planting our food, witnessing the flowers
of the trees turning into fruits, for us
communities graced to eat these staple crops
in the Philippines, the exposure
to such grace and wonders
can't help but to entertain questions such as,
"Why is the mango shaped as a heart?"

Wave No More Goodbyes

The innocent smiles
The well-hidden pain and tears
Cradled by the Pacific Ocean
Wave hello to me, wave no more goodbyes

From above the clouds, and much rain
From above, are the unknown heavens
Of stars and guiding lights
Of hidden treasures and wonders

Across This Vast Ocean

Across this vast ocean.
Far far away.
Across the Pacific Ocean.
The largest ocean in the world.
Is Home.
Across this mind and imaginations,
Visions and dreams stalled.
Across this time. Holds the past,
Present and the future.
In trusting this Life and the world
This world with fingers so rough
In trusting and asking questions
Is it with, or without repercussions?
When are we safe? Is it worth it?
When are we allowed to live our lives?
In dignity, happiness, and in peace.

Time is Invisible Gold

Time is gold
Time which we take for granted
Time which the greed exploit us with
Time which leaves our body and soul
To perish
We are the young and the restless
We are the visions of the past
The dignified youth,
The valor and the sacrifices

In Holding

In this beautiful struggle we call Life
The beauty and the wonders that seem no end
Leaving us with the pieces of the broken hearts

Holding,
Praying in our knees,
Asking for the strength
To carry on
That if the end come marching,
May we be rightful and strong

Horizon - What Is?

We are surrounded with technology,
Education, Models, and Scholars
What philosophy do we need?
What does the world need?
And who?
We spend time after time, thinking,
Reaching, achieving
What is in the horizon
Losing each second,
Time is ticking

Waiting For

I always dream of paradise.
Of the wonders.
Of the lost world
Of the past civilizations' dreams

Broken and promised
A broken promise
That came unspoken

We are our ancestors' wildest
Wildest dreams!
We are the ones we have been
Waiting for.

When Not Fooled

The masses is you and I, the common people,
The subjects of other peoples' subjects,
experiments,
And whatever more, being pulled like chess
pawns
Among the masses are truly good people, good
hearts, Good souls, yet damned when wishing to
question,
When not converted, recruited, or fooled,
When poor, sick, traumatized, refusing to be
sold
When violated by gnawing politicians, yelled &
belittled
When violated by the cops, arrested, kicked and
kneed
Only fine when palatable to the mould, whose
mould?
When over milking the milked, until there is no
milk left
When not fitting as a perk, a maid, a fund, a
material
And more, what more? How long and why
more?
Afterall, after all these, the masses remain,
standing

Power True

True power never sprouted, reproduced,
organised
By the cowards, who hide behind that red book
shields
Who walk red carpets with their lovers and
accolades,
Sowing brokeness in the lands with their dirty
hands
It's the people without the above privileges,
Who work hard, toil hard, fight hard, love hard
Breaking generational curses, in love & struggle,
And in true meaning of sacrifice.
Thus, diversity and inclusion are then realised
On kinship, not all things are the same, not the
same
We do not bleed and suffer the same.

Vultures

In the vast, and across oceans, and lands far
away,
Groups, gangs, cults---history erasers, follow us
here
Who but unite, aim to erase, outdo others.
Fascism?
Who colonised others, gang up against one &
others
Who remain colonists, who exist against the
others,
What better days, what revolutionary hey days,
When our youth, visions stolen? By so-called
leaders
Who lure the young, to force feed what, whose
process
To trust, to compromise, then taken advantage,
Since when is it ever safe and allowed,
To question our politicians, self-hailed, narcs
Is it sin to doubt leaders as Leaders,
Doubt elders as Elders, teachers as Teachers?
When there are fake healers, fake culture
keepers
Groups protecting those who erase, and colonise
As they also raise their wrists up in the crowds,
Some of us may be still too young to understand

To process, but taken advantage, eaten
In the process, of losing our young, our time.

Who Is Your Saviour?

"Who will save us as the world tears itself to
shreds?
As speculation and fear of what shall or should
Have been done only increases, global crises
continue
And persist. Our current situation sheds light
On the fragility of our safety and welfare.
We are products of systemic racism
And economic inequality - we are products
Of tradition and history.
Who is Your Saviour and how can they help
me?"